Artist Calling

Expressionism Photography

Copyright © 2018 by Dana Gregory

All rights reserved. No part of this book may be reproduced, scanned, or distributed in any printed or electronic form without permission

First Edition July 2018

Printed in the United States of America

Preface

"Don't ask yourself what the world needs, ask yourself what makes you come alive. And then go do that. Because what the world needs are people who have come alive." -Harold Whitman

The journey of becoming an artist is experiencing the lows and the highs with the movements forward but also knowing what captures your heart in that moment and when you begin to come alive inside. Each step of self-exploring is the delicate process one must endure to find where the art meets the artist and the artist finds an accelerating treasure within their own heart. This is when the artist begins to race the clock for that experience of being in the moment. It's then, when the artist knows there is a channel of wisdom to share with the world and expresses it through the art format.

It's the inward spin of knowing the reality can meet you in the inner world of your own imagination, but you capture it with the way, you need to express the journey inward out to others. It is when the artist can share the story from the perceptions of what is seen and heard but through the artists lens. This is when the mind goes through many potential expressions within the field of creativity.

Opening and letting go as an artist is a scary step from the levels of beginnings and then each moment one explores outside of the normal. These questions run through heart and soul of the artist." Am I good enough?"   Are people going to love or hate my work?" and so, I have to understand the layers of the art world. Not all art fits in the glove of all humans but every glove can fit in the hands of the maker.

The artist calling is special way of thinking through art from a different Psychology point of view but also, showing how to come alive, when the soul has endeavored something hard in this lifetime. It's the sharing part that makes the artist want to reach out and give the heart and soul of their art through the soul experience of making the art.

There are numerous of ways one can explore the depths of the universe and earth, but it is the process of capture and release for the artist. It becomes a challenging moment of what is good and what is not, when exploring the avenues of acceptance. I have come to terms with this angle and this is just become alive and make a statement with art and show the world what you have seen and felt as, an artist.

Carrying the load of un-acceptable is to heavy these days. So go out and explore the world and give what you see and feel from your own perceptions and then, watch people grow and blossom with the expressions of art through life.

Artists Calling

Expressionism Photography

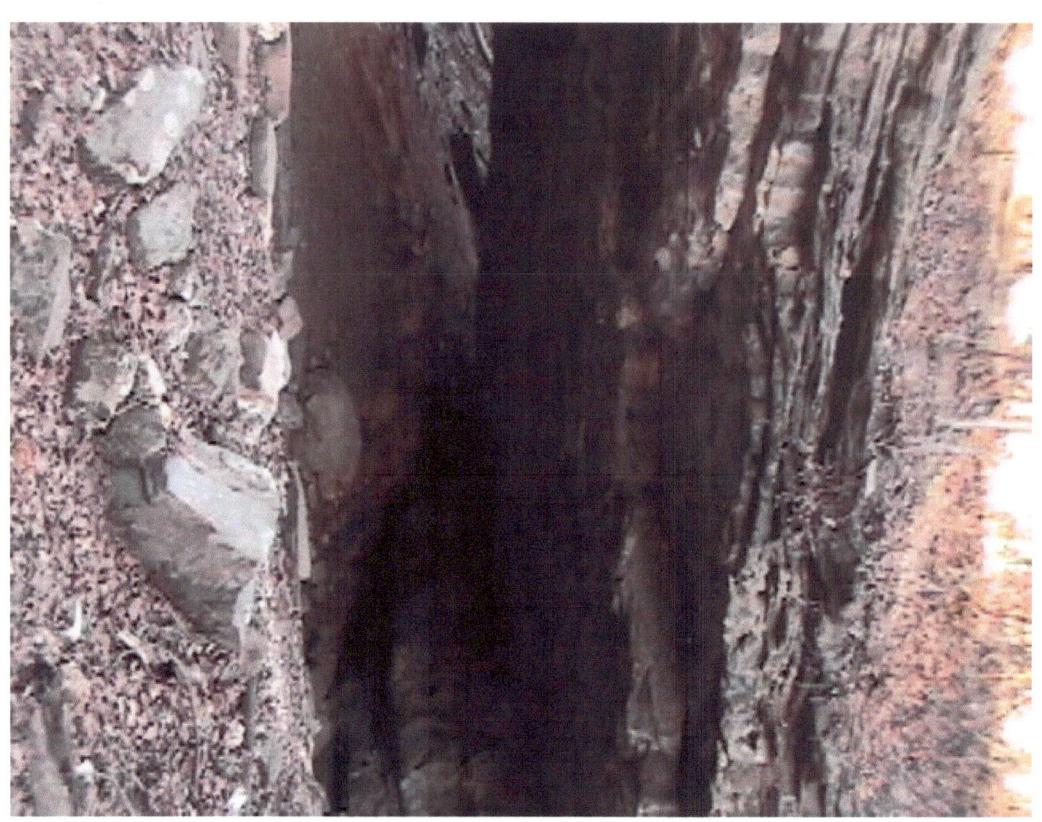

Physical Desire Split from the Soul's Desire

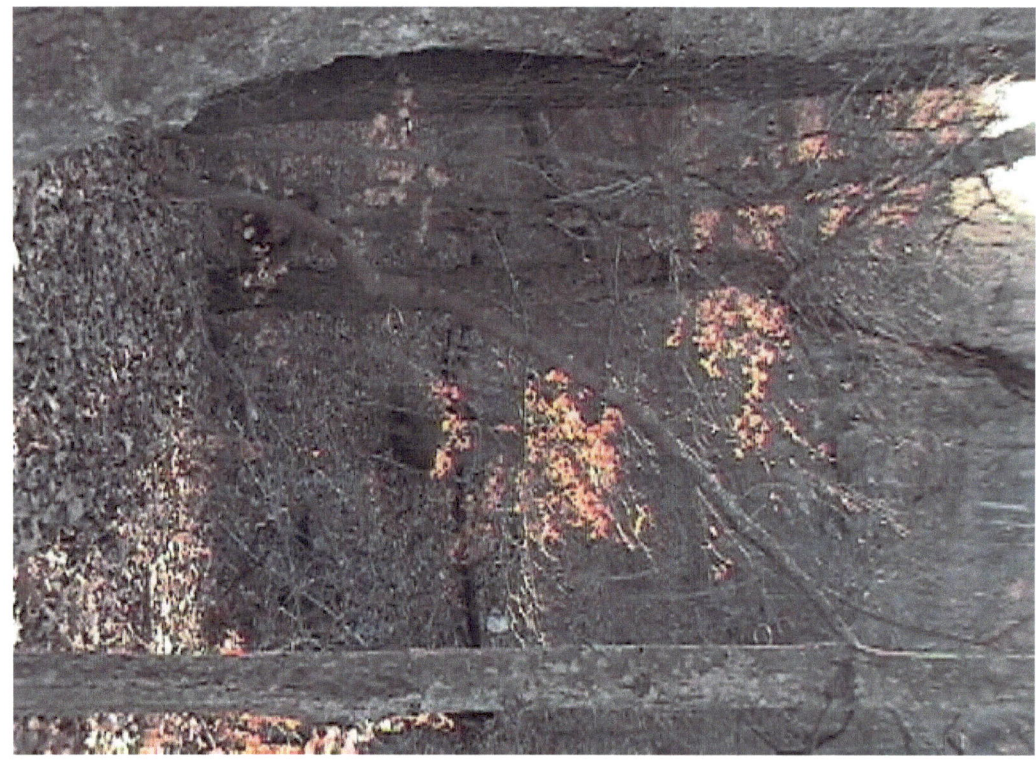

Touching the Edges

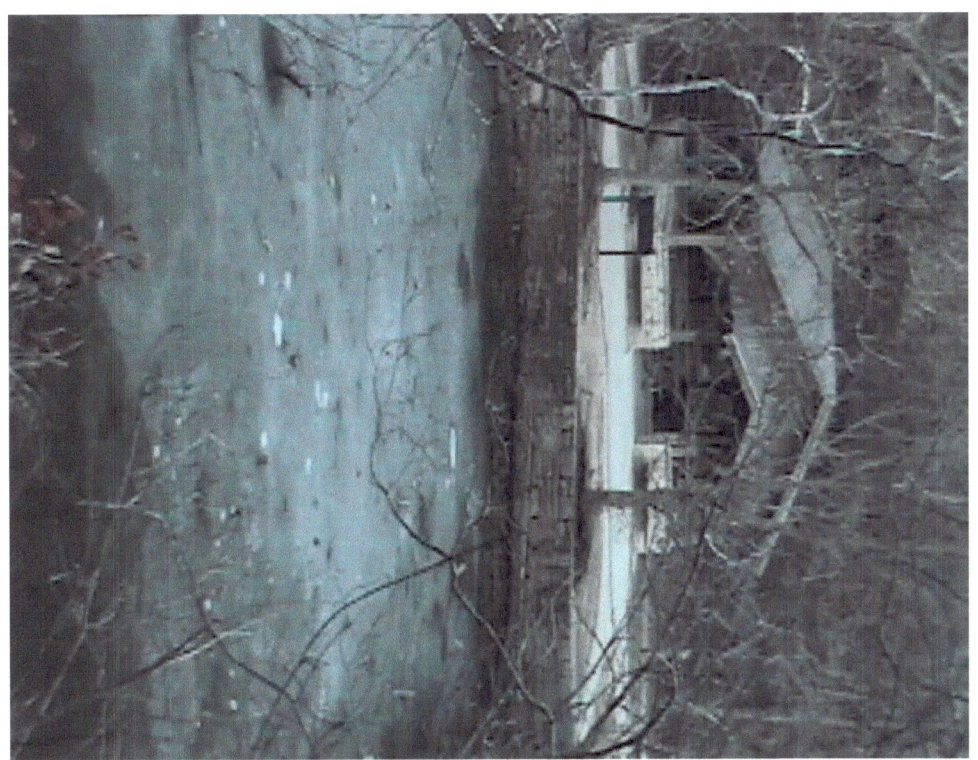

Frozen Comfort

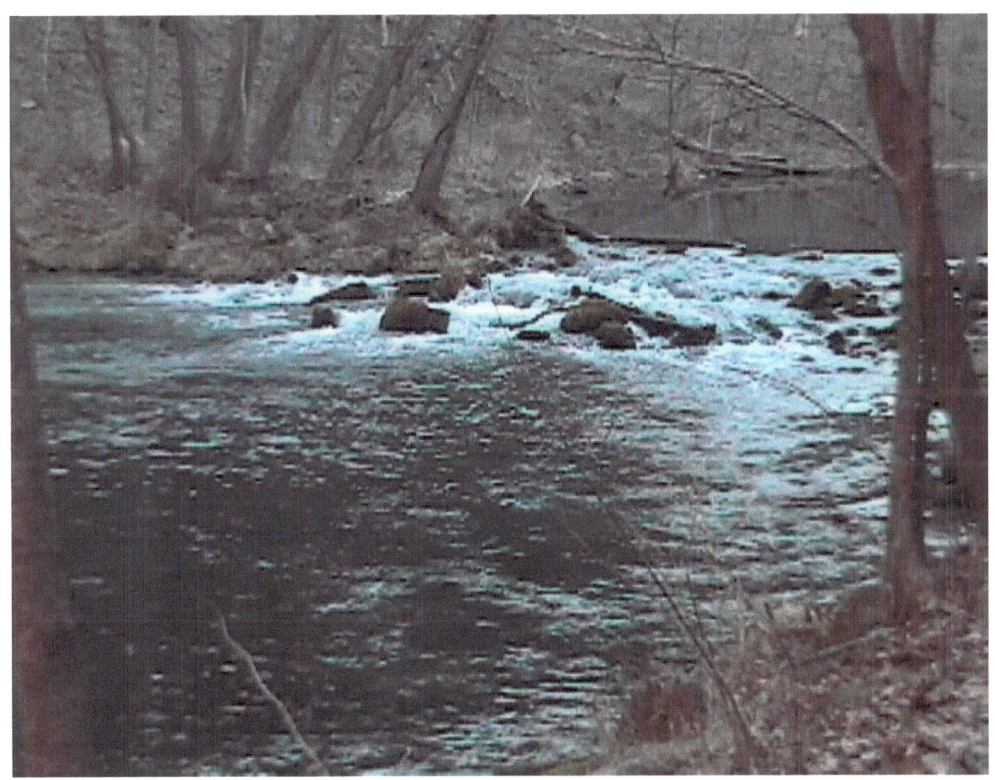

Desire within Distance

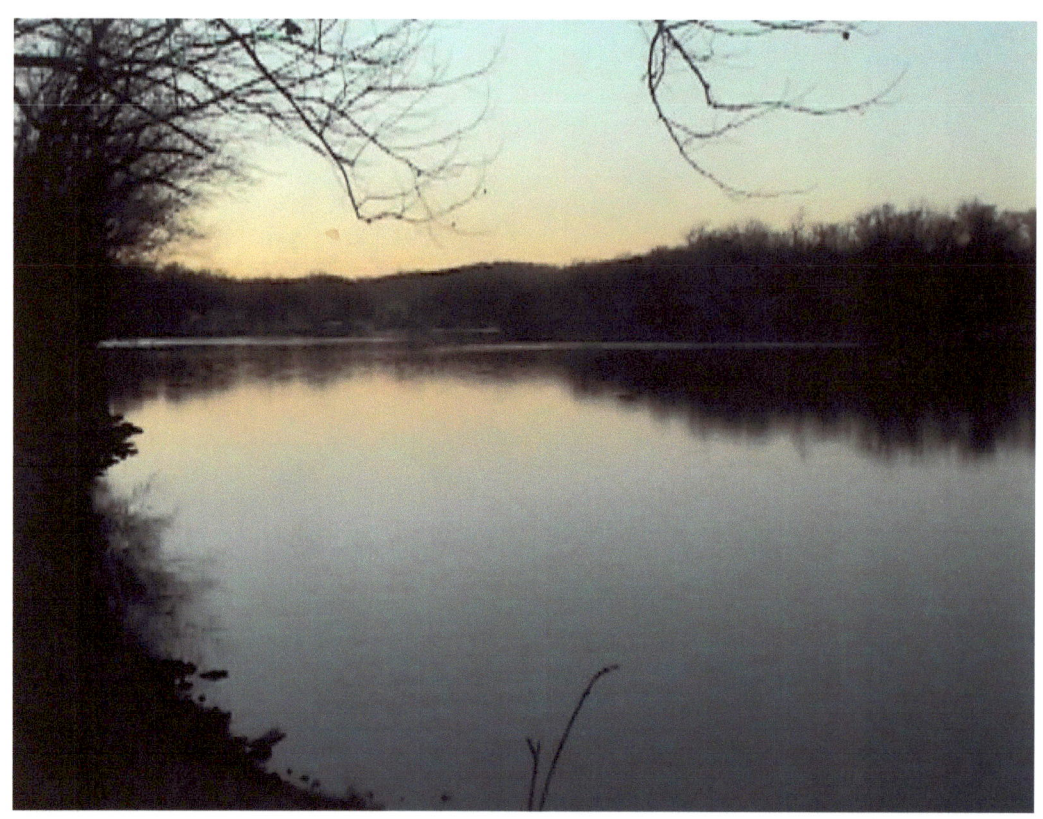

Calmness

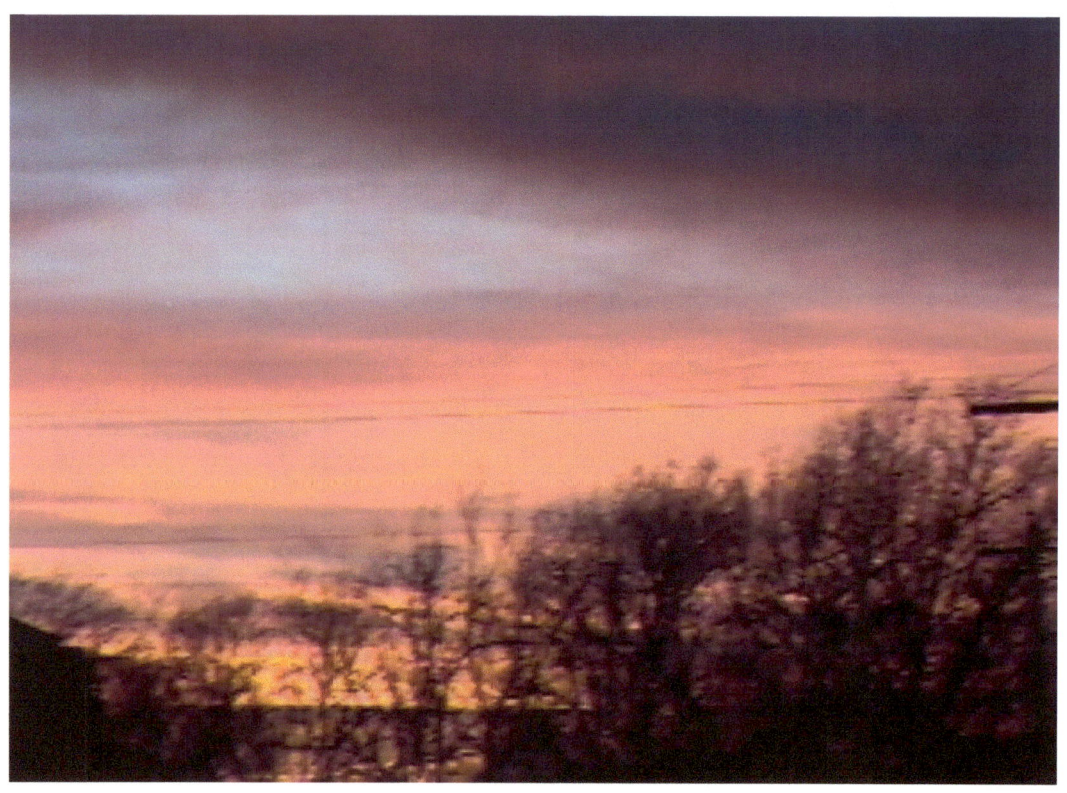

Good Morning America

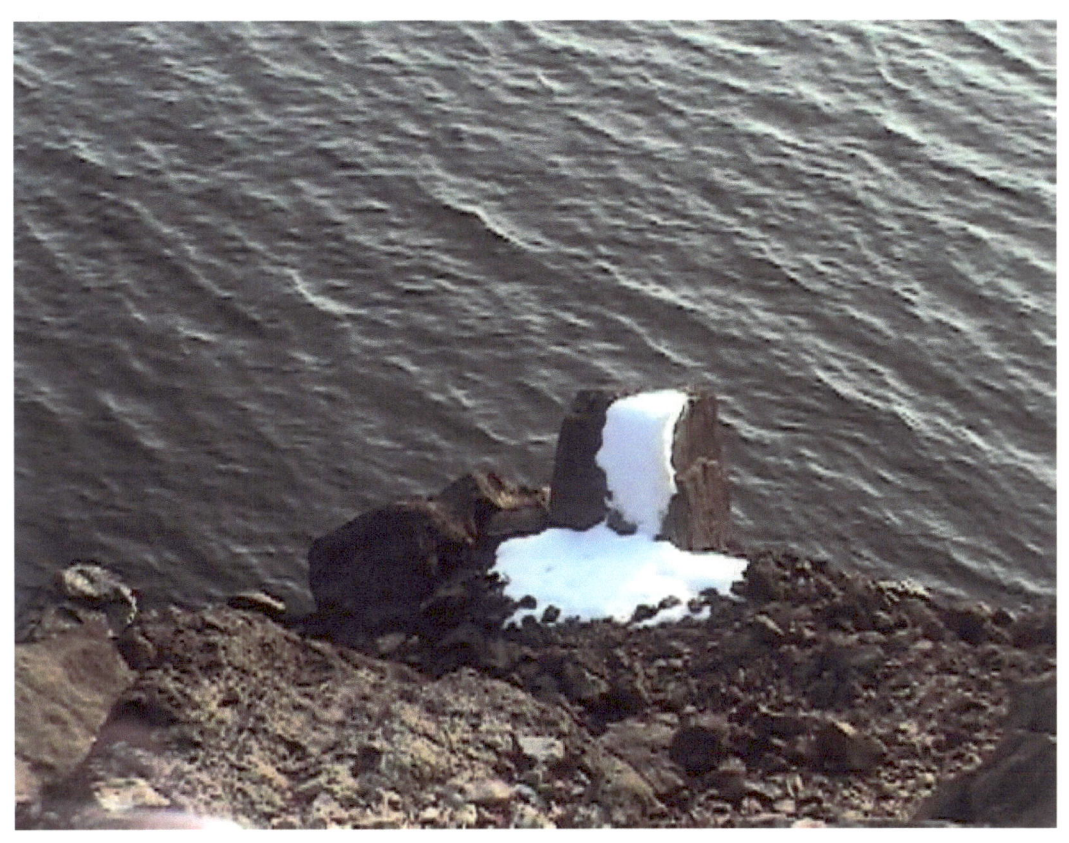
Un-Thawing Emotional Trauma

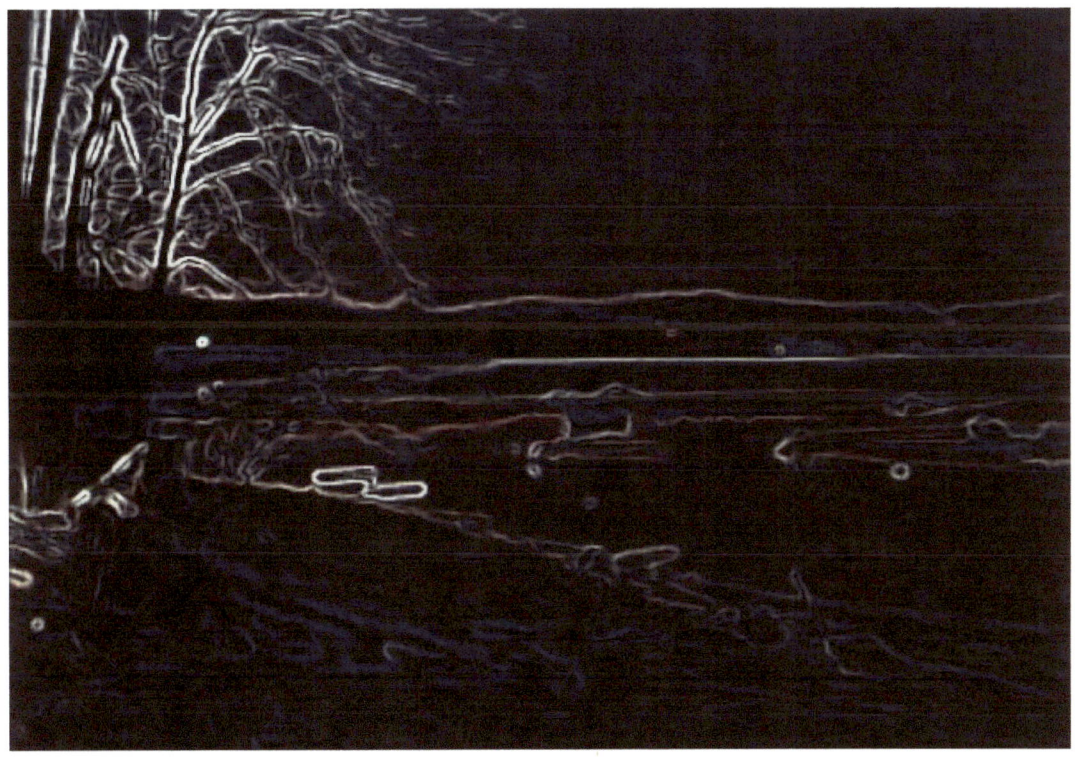
Edges

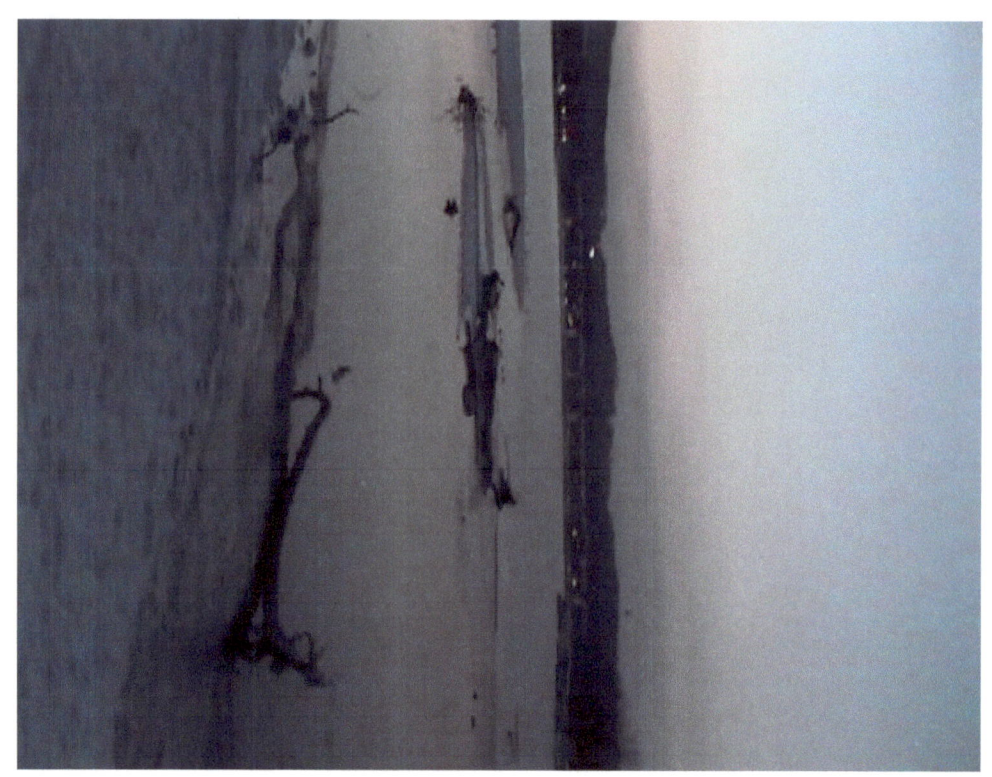

Surrendering to the Center of the Inner Child

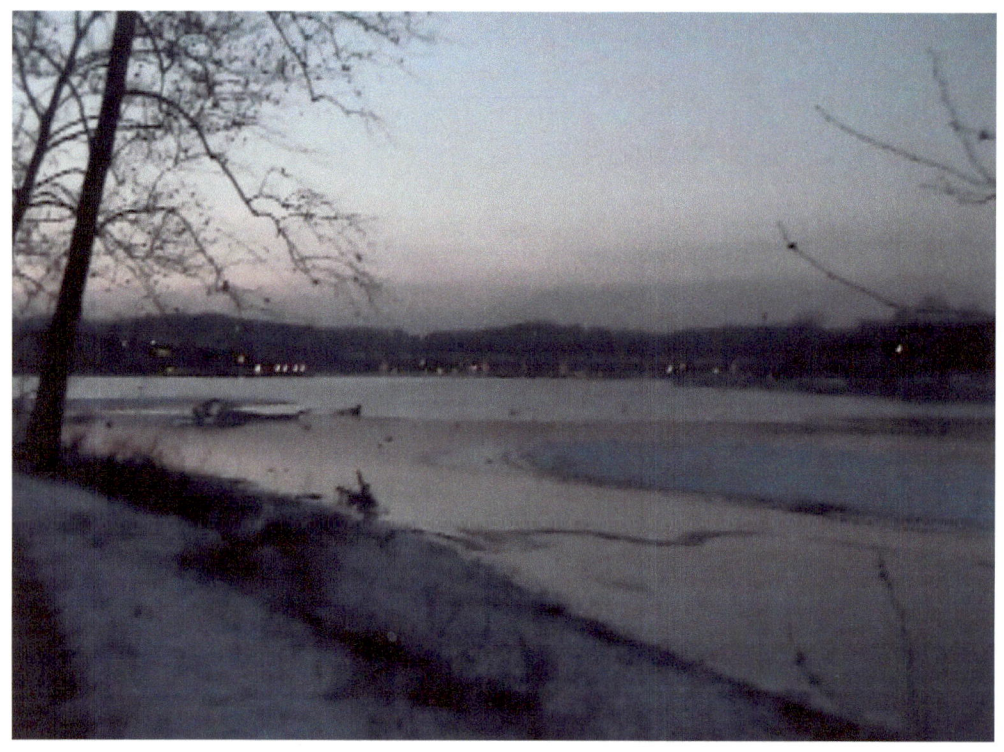

Sensations of Cold Breeze

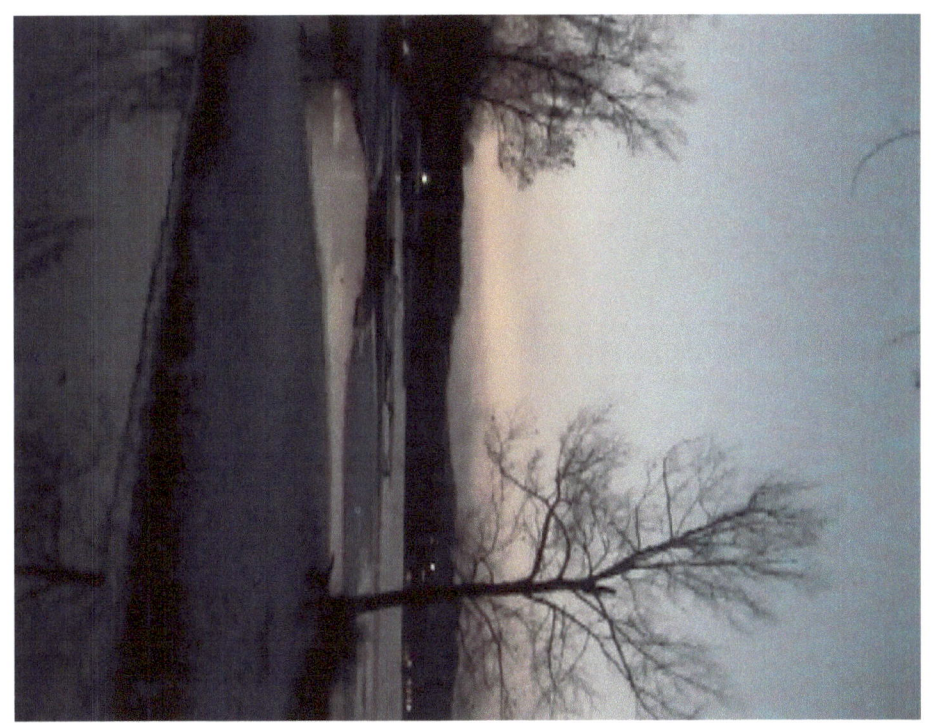

Tilted Love and Compassion

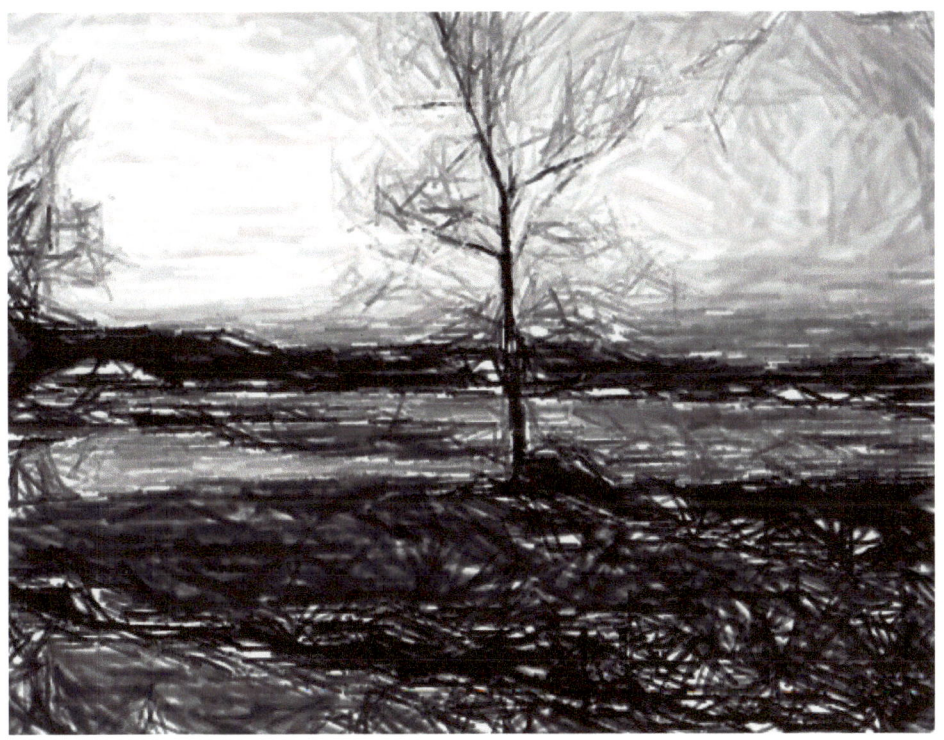

Self-Leader with Ideas

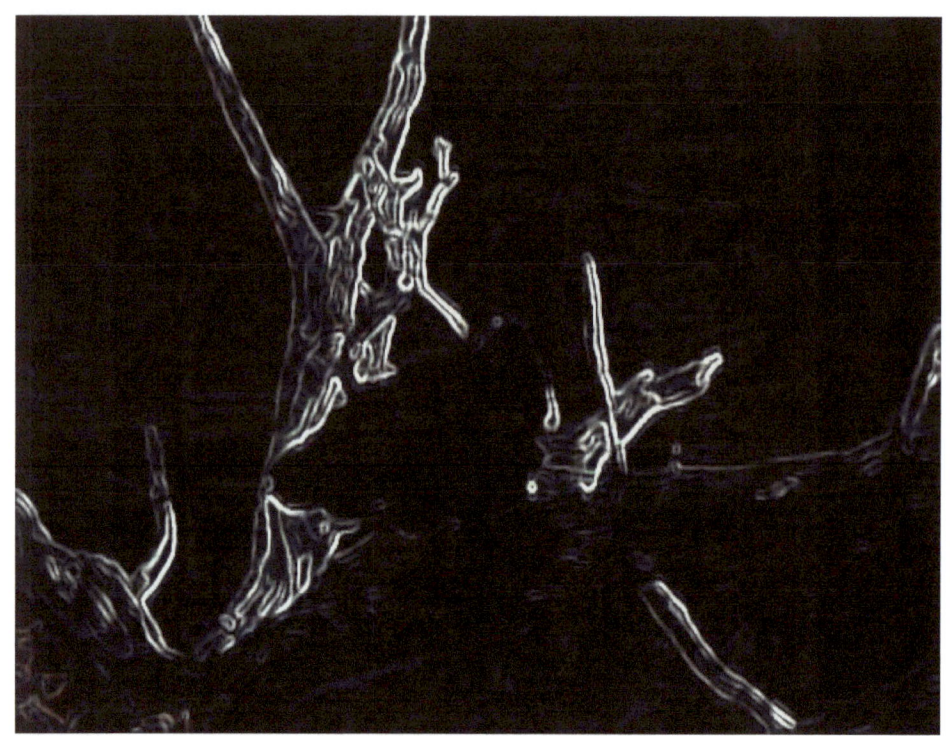

Self-Reliance

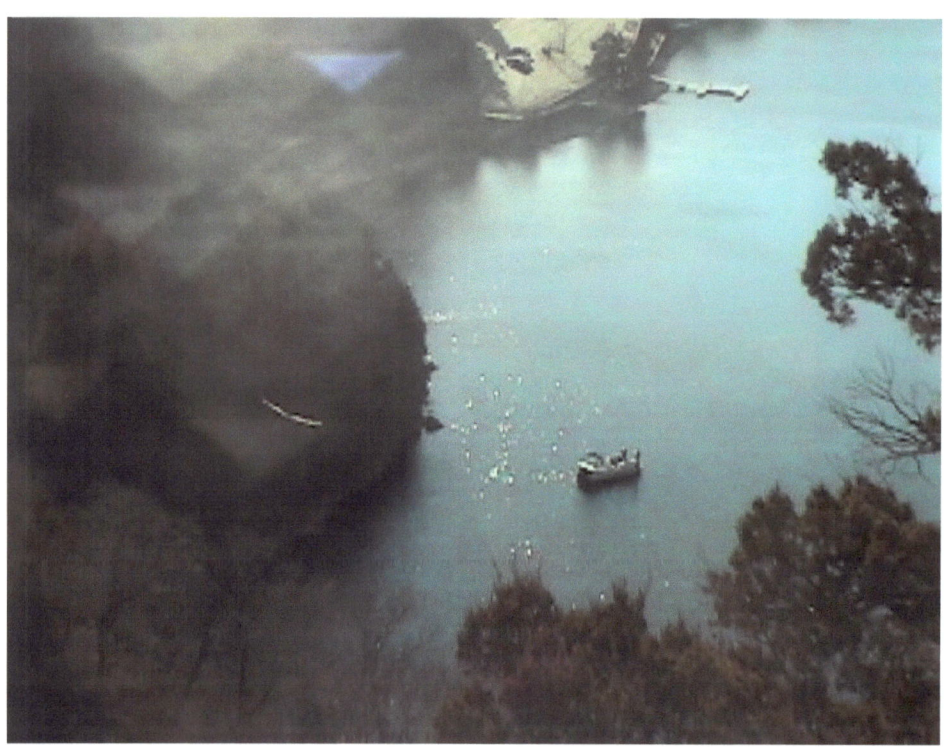

Foggy Distance of Remembrance of Achievements

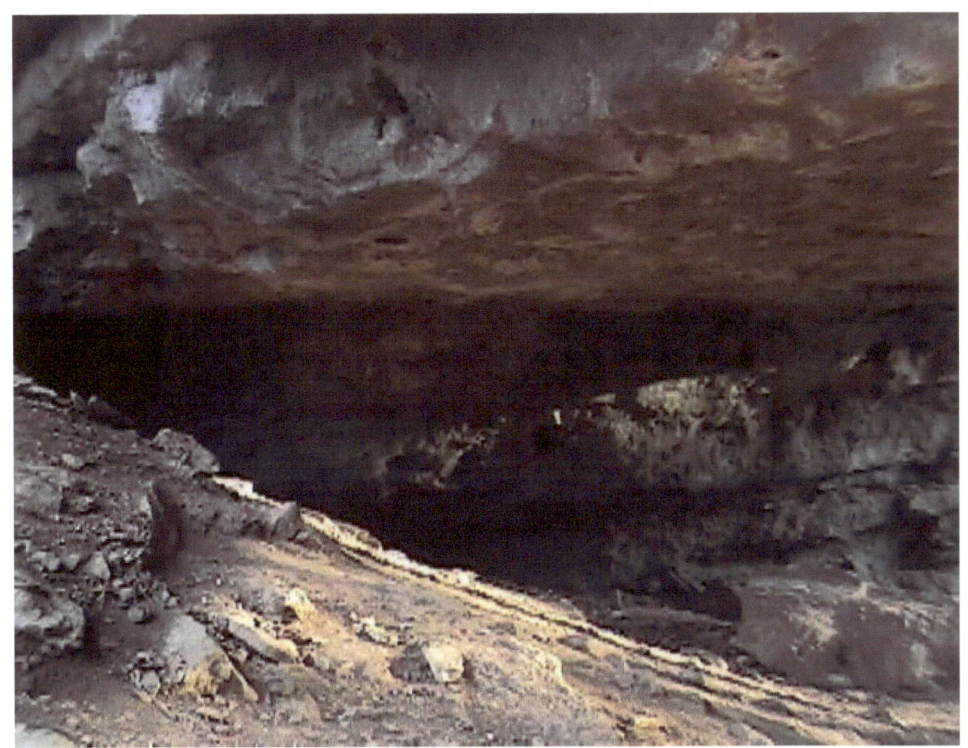

Climbing In

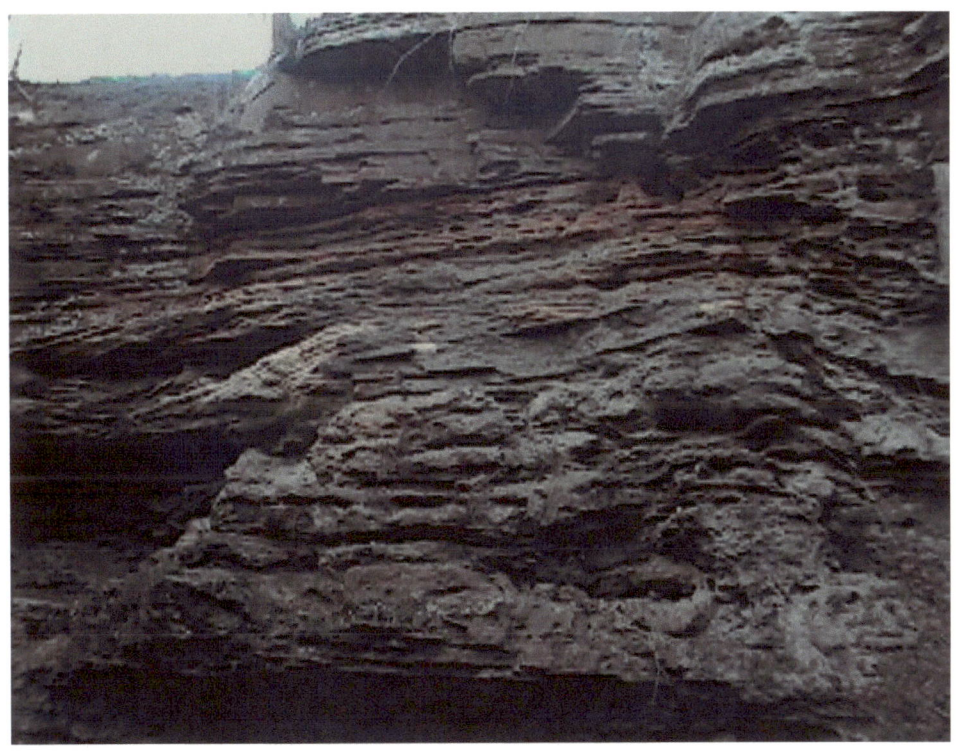

Strategy of Forging Forward

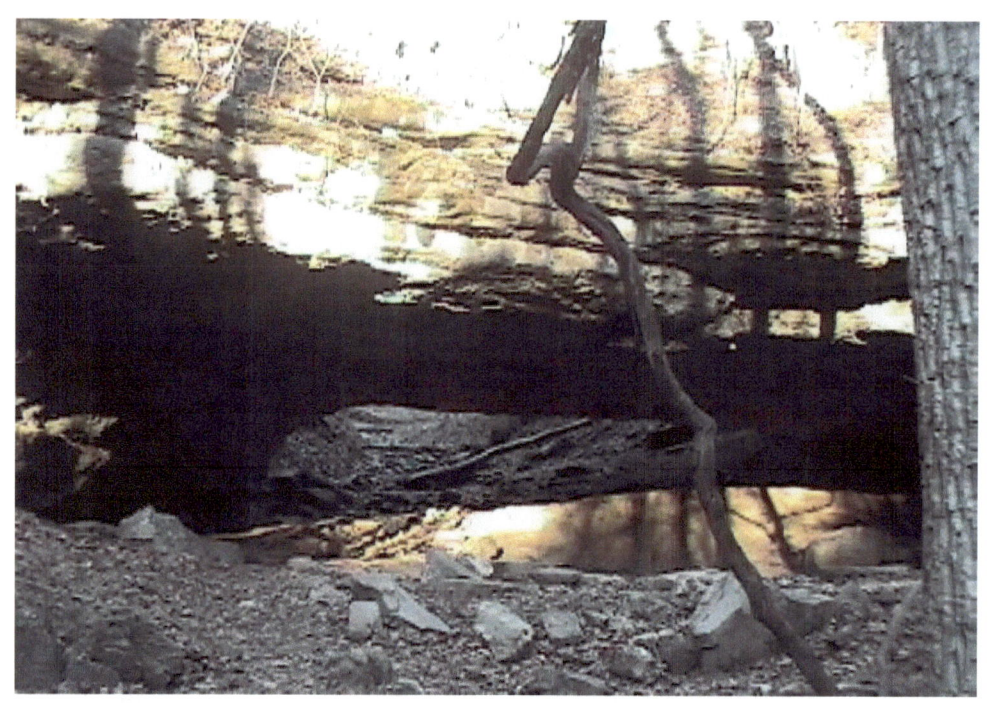

Over-Seeing Possibilities

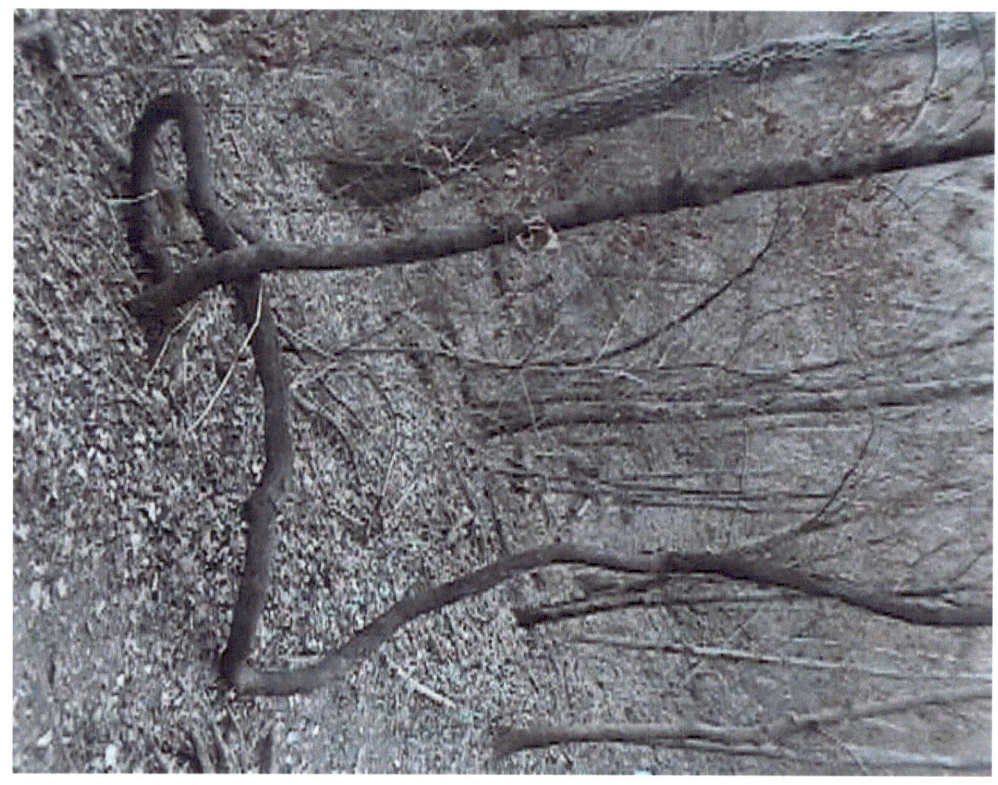

Grey analogy with Curves

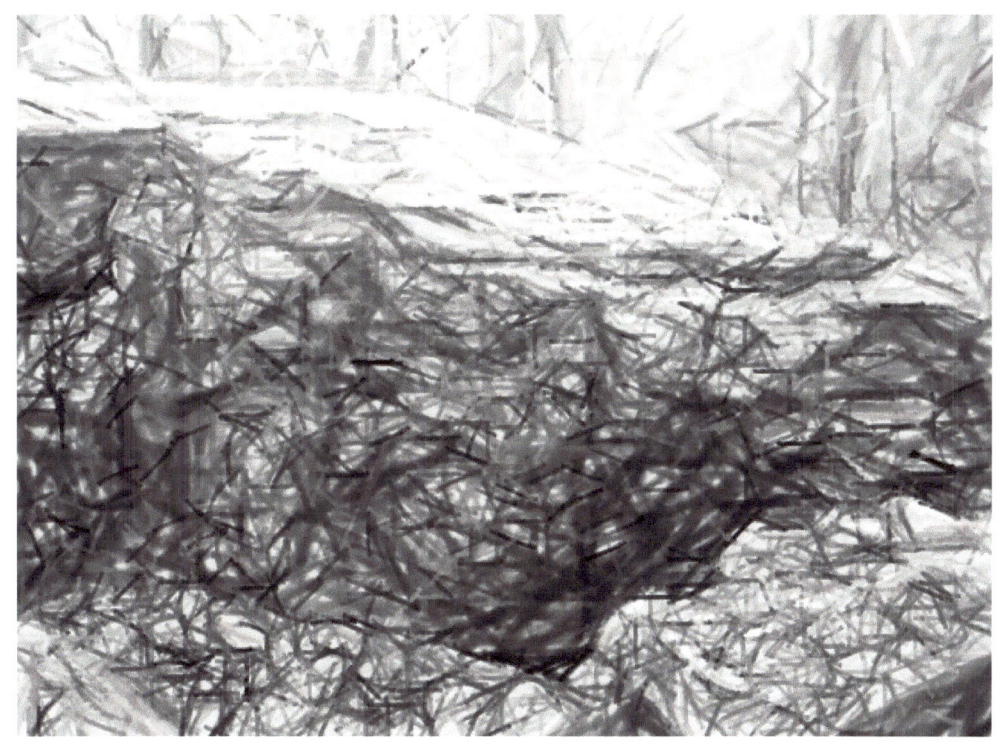

Resting Within

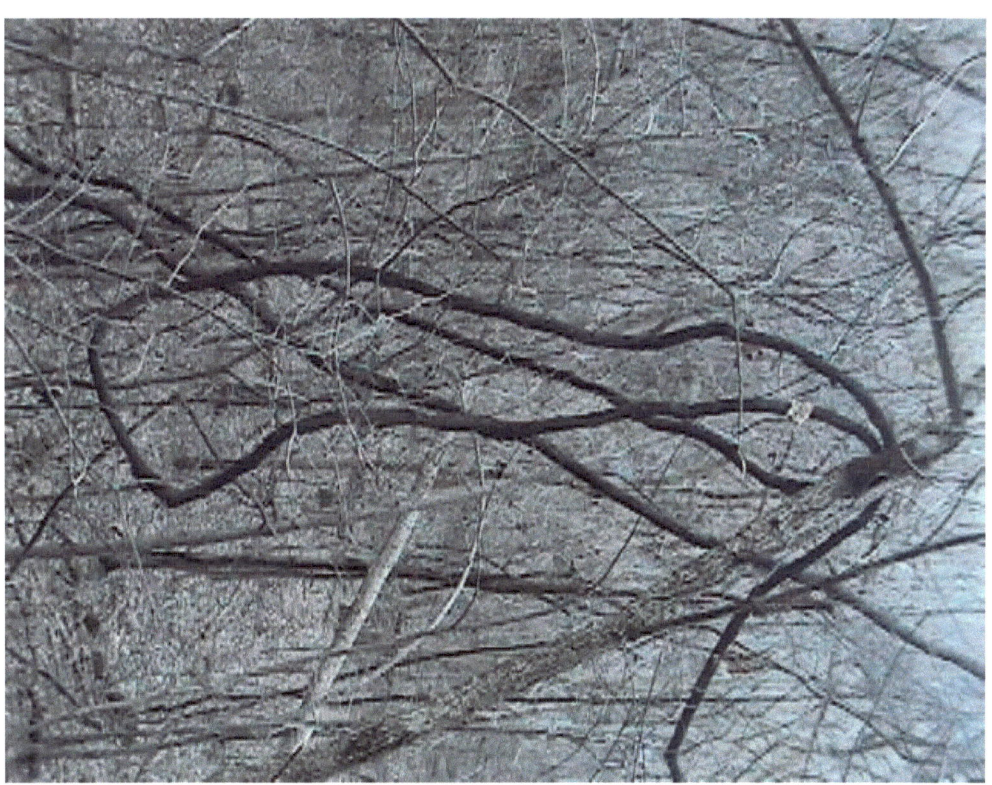

Unity

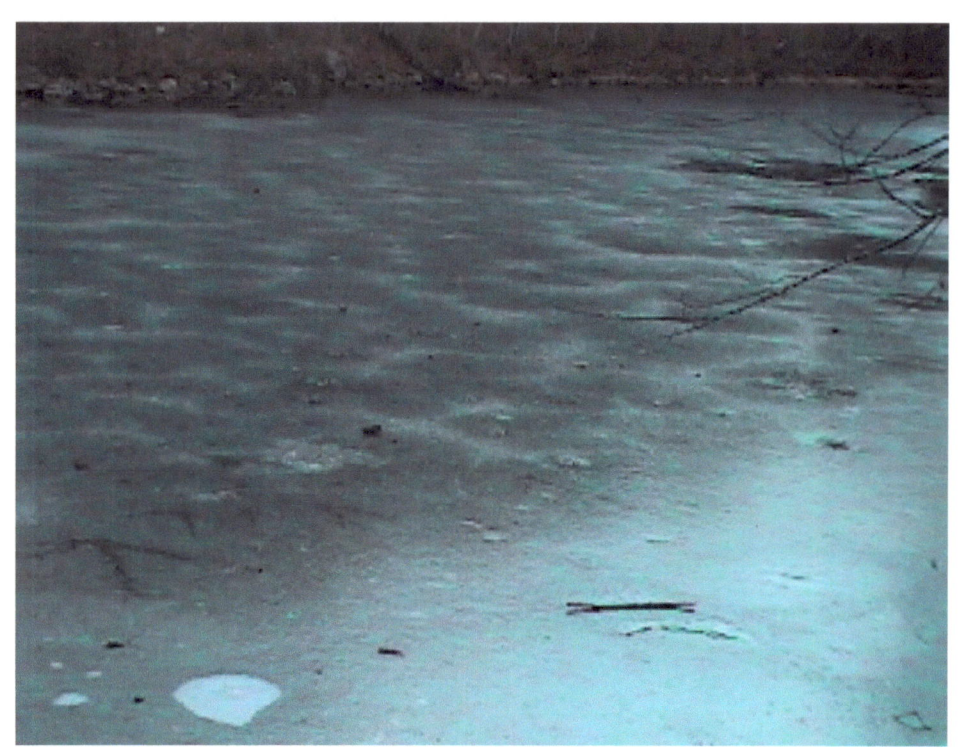

Frozen Words of a Child

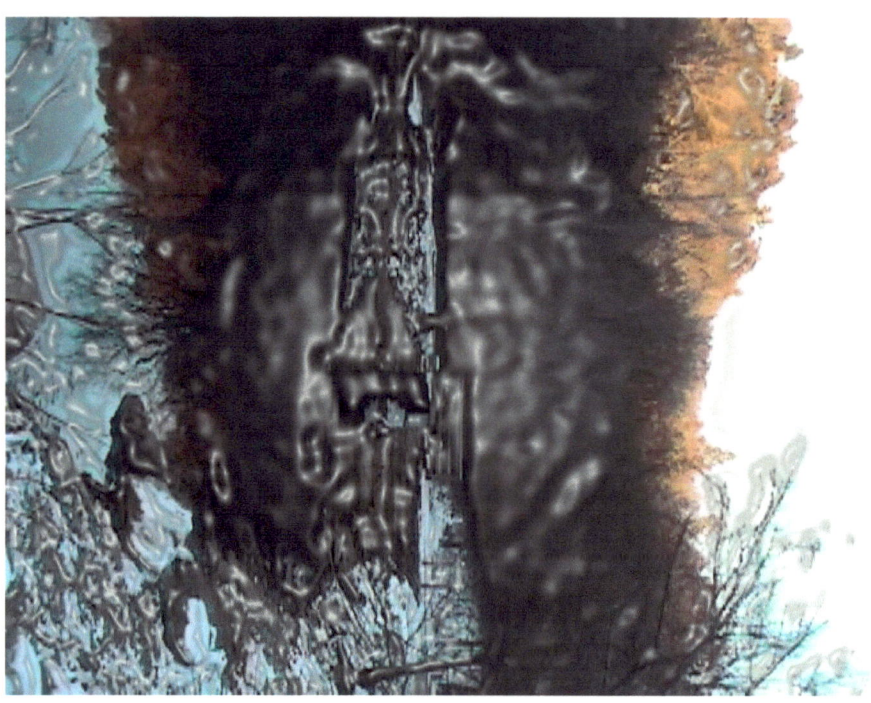

Melted in Nature

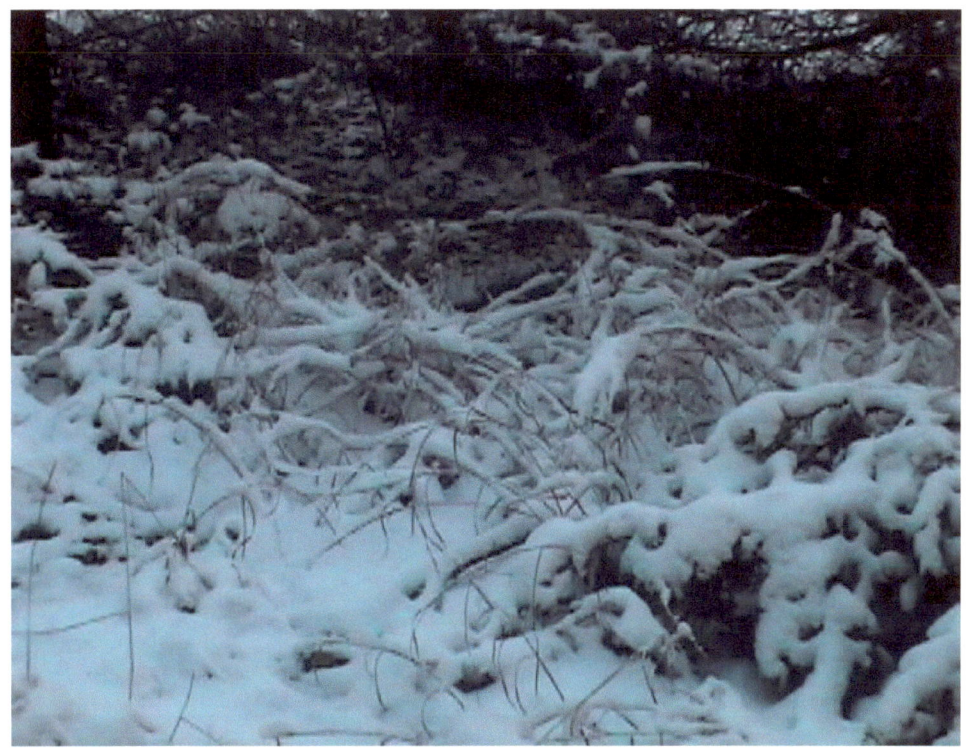

Christmas Feeling

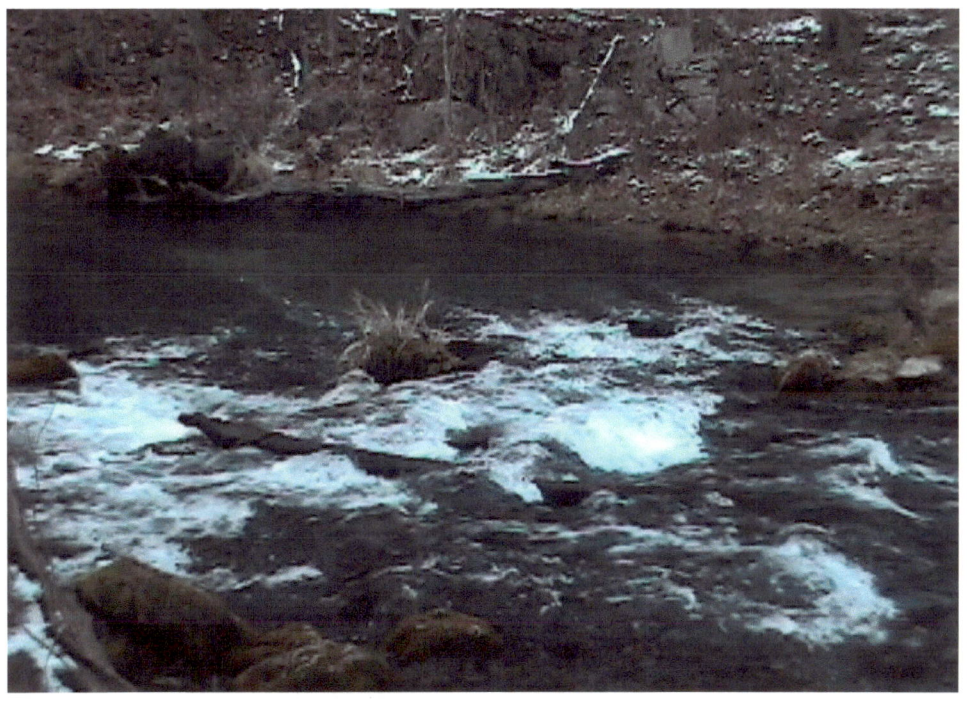

Earth Flowing

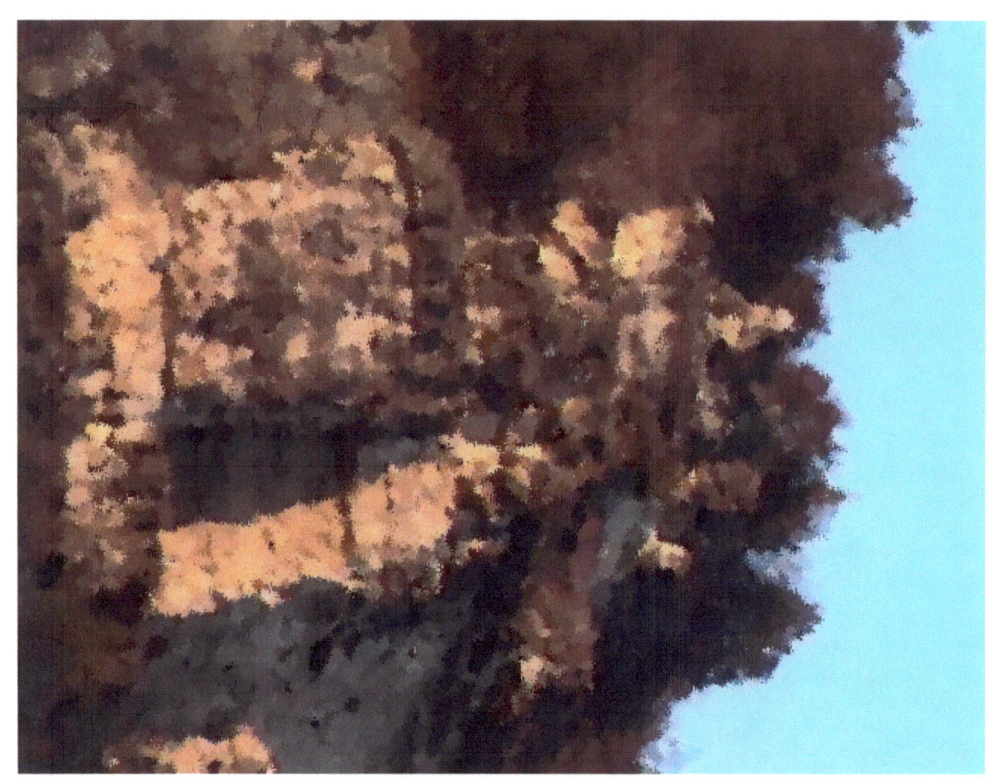

Strength Within Creativity

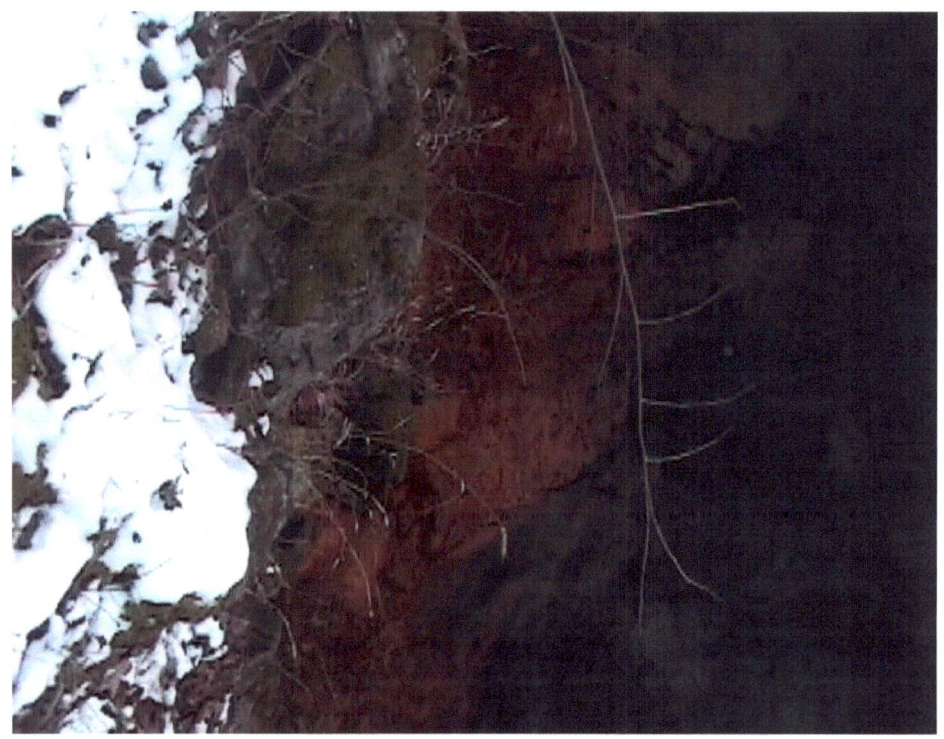

Earthy Moment

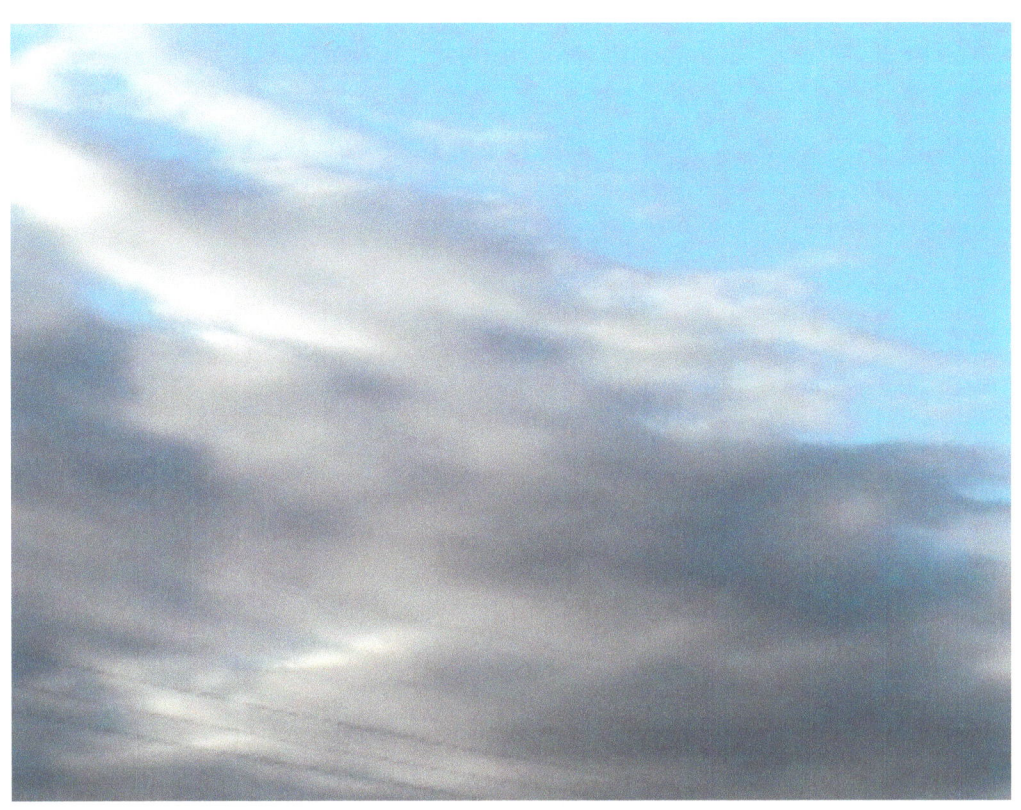

Freedom Within Business

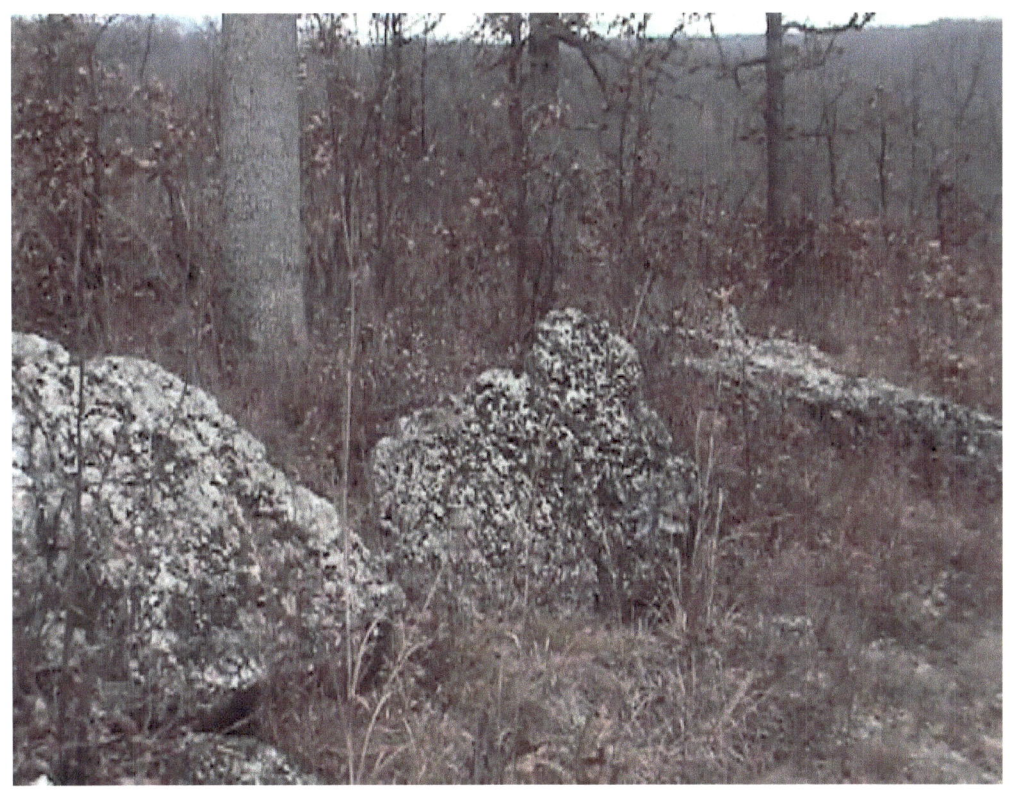

Structure

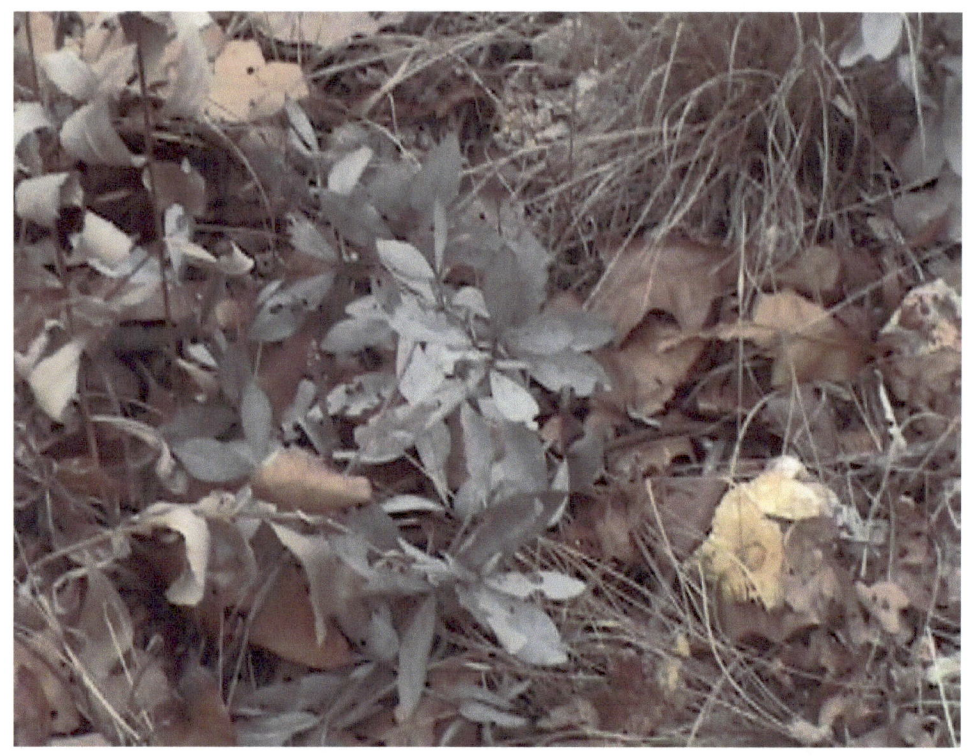

Engagement

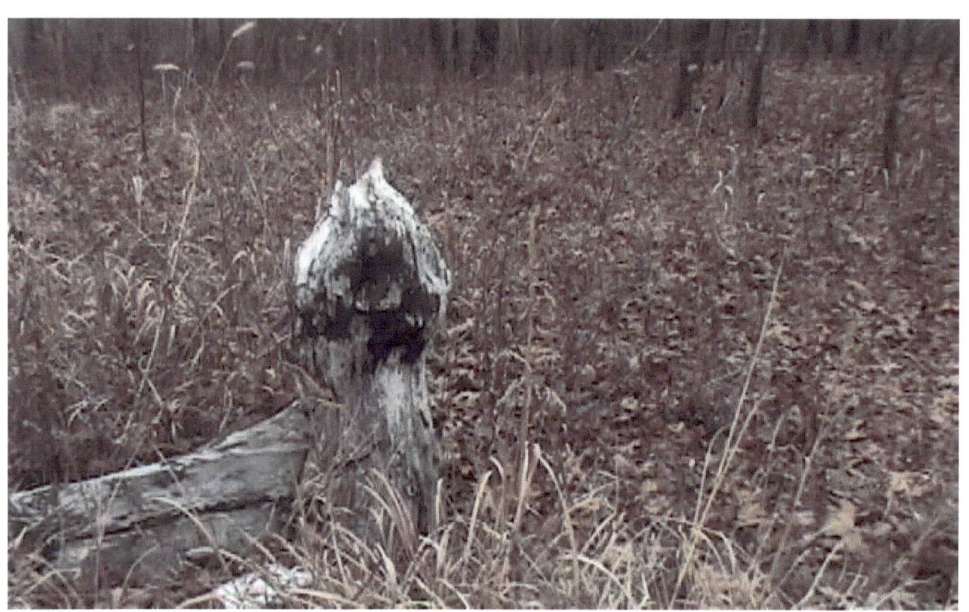

Experience

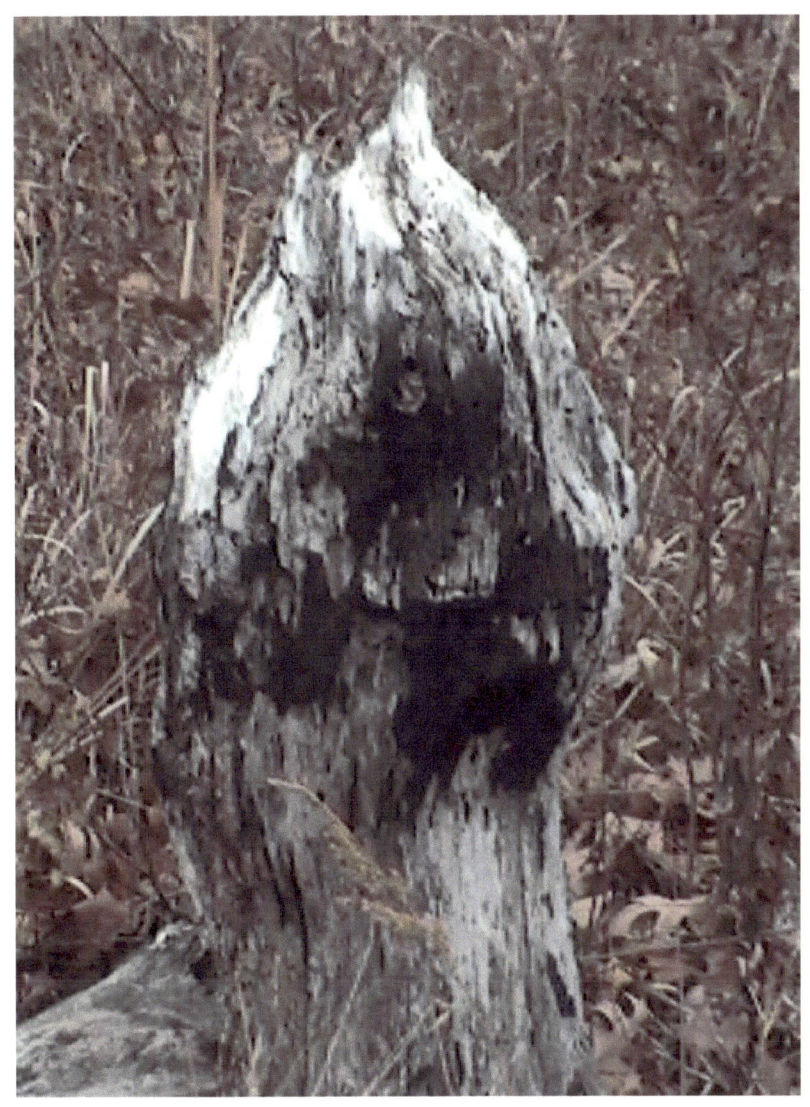

Story Telling

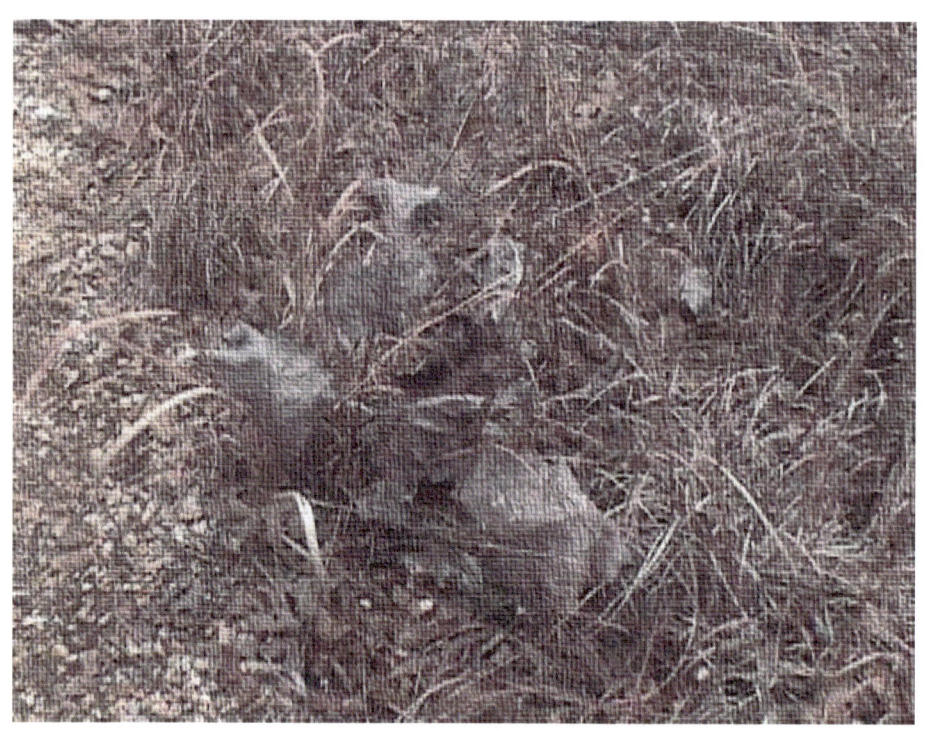
Texture Thinking

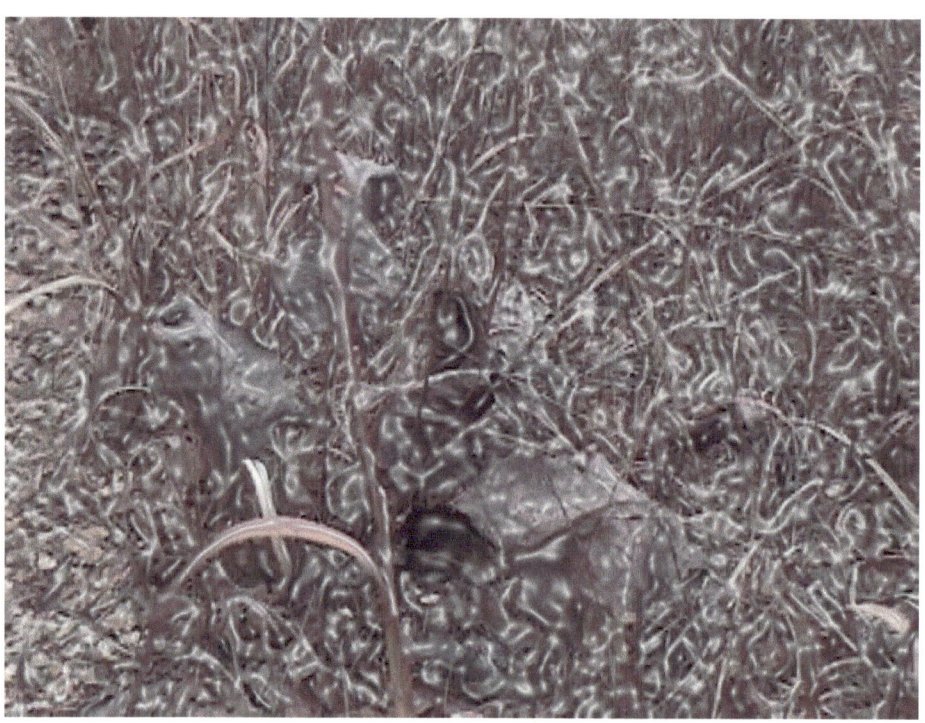
Sensations Molded Within

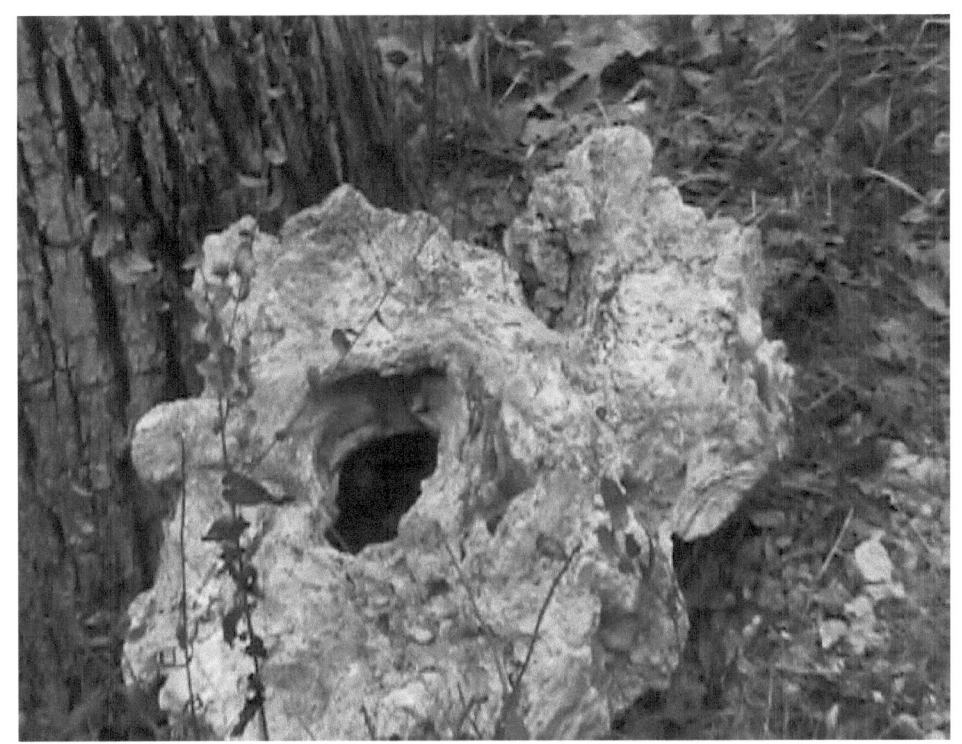

Collective Piece

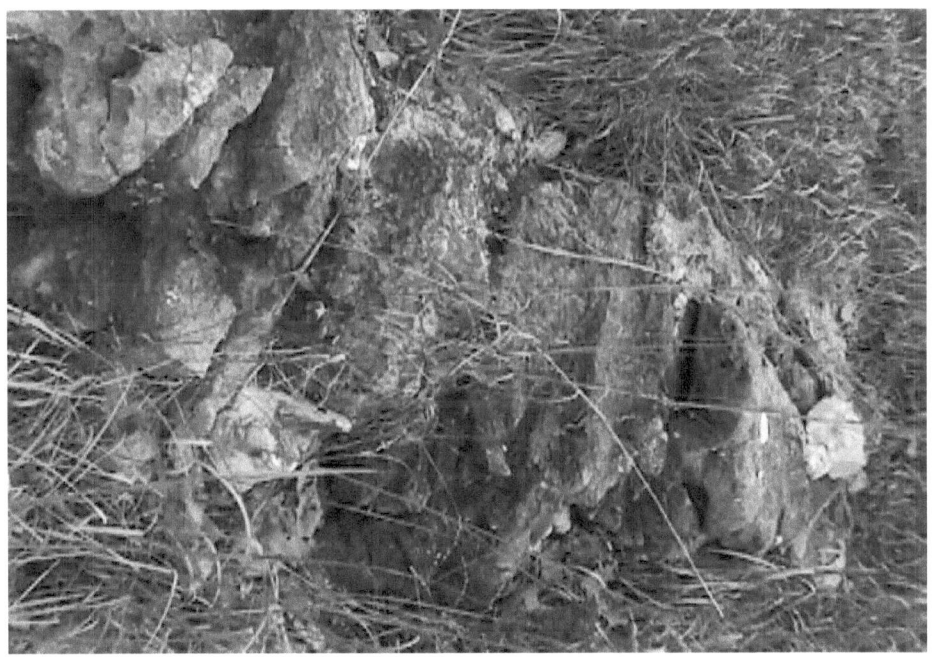

Heaviness

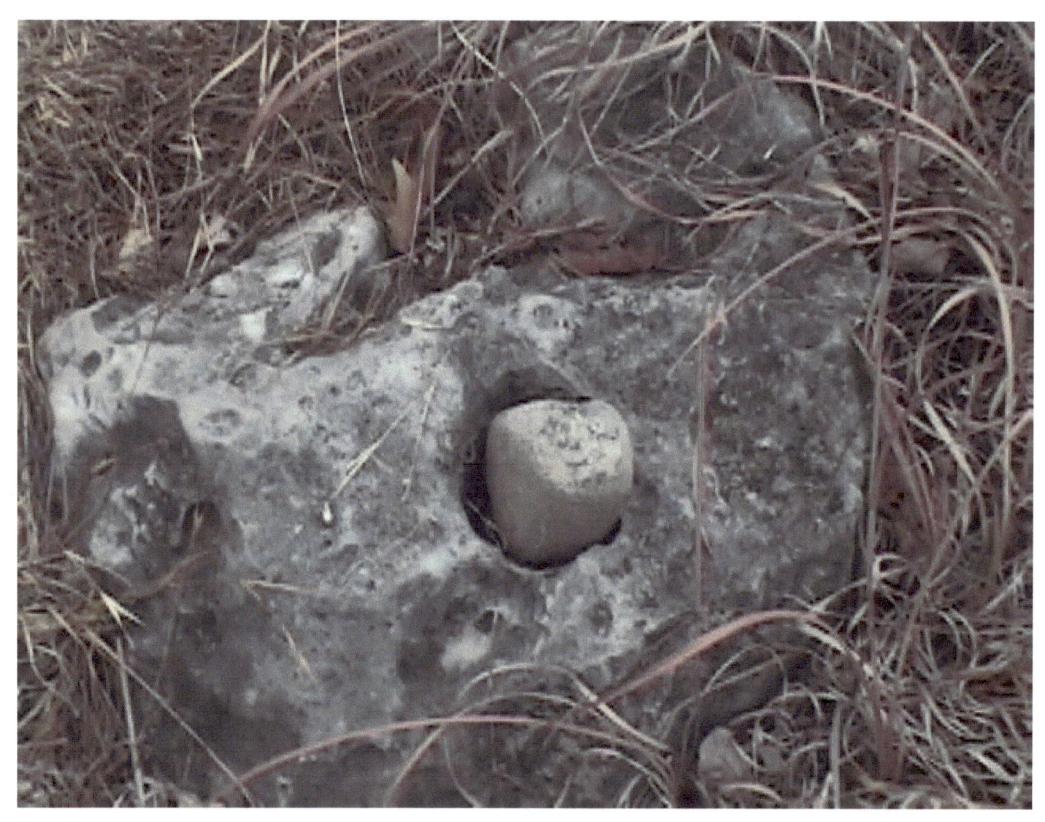

Abstract thinking "I'm Finding Holes in Earth and Solving the Problem"

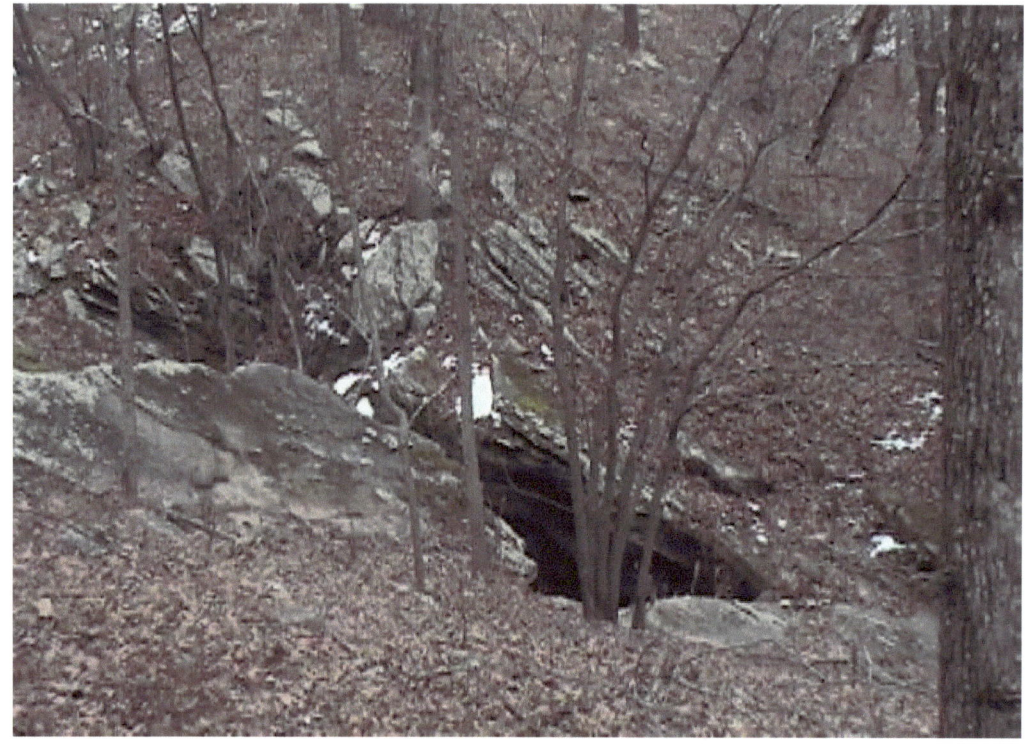

Diving In

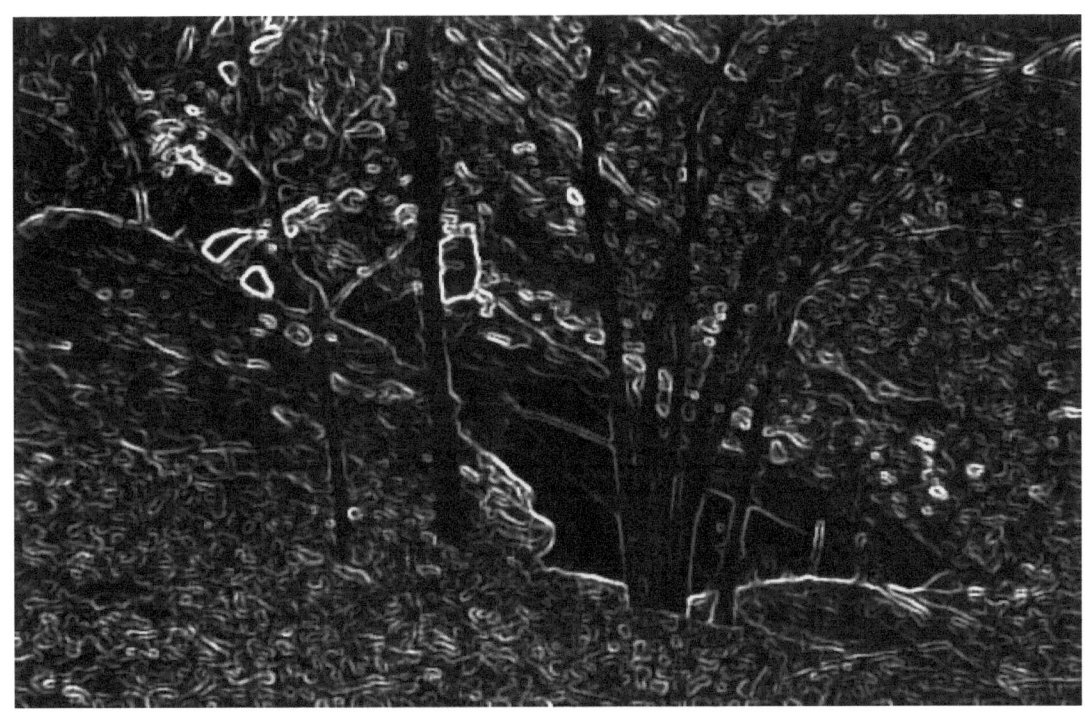

Challenge of Integrative Thinking

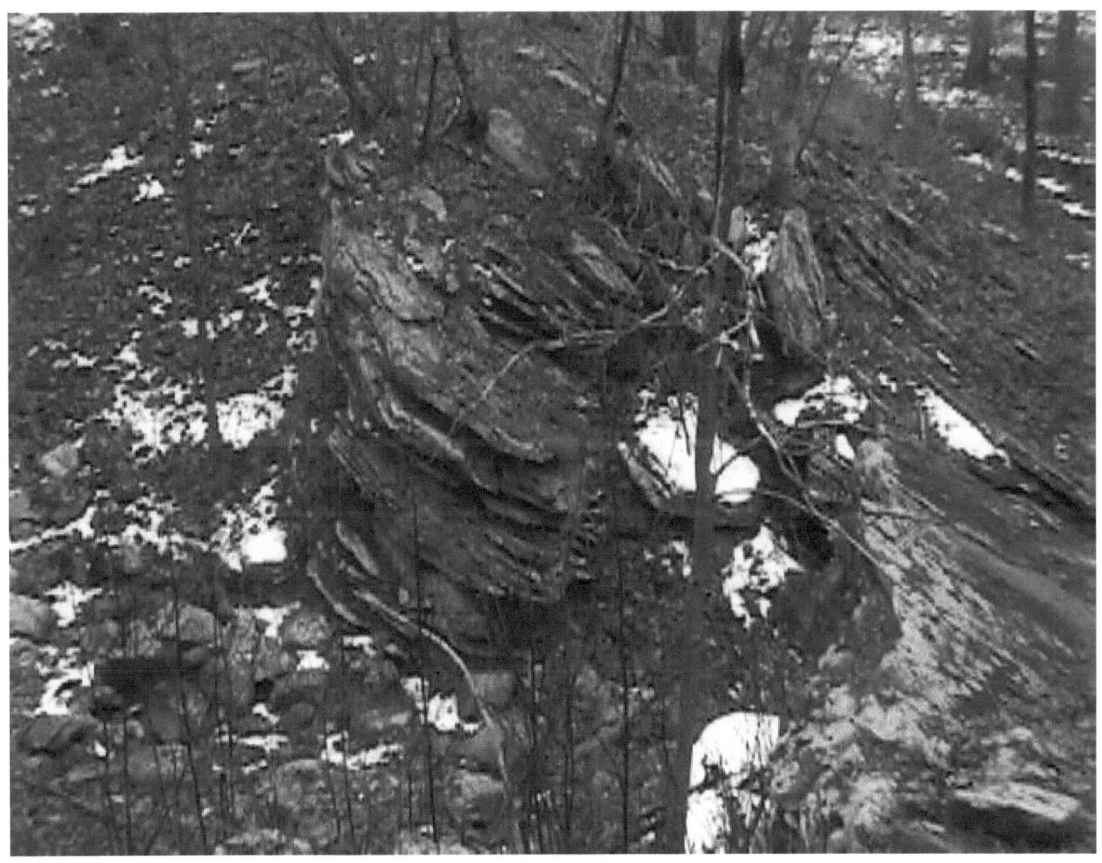

Observation

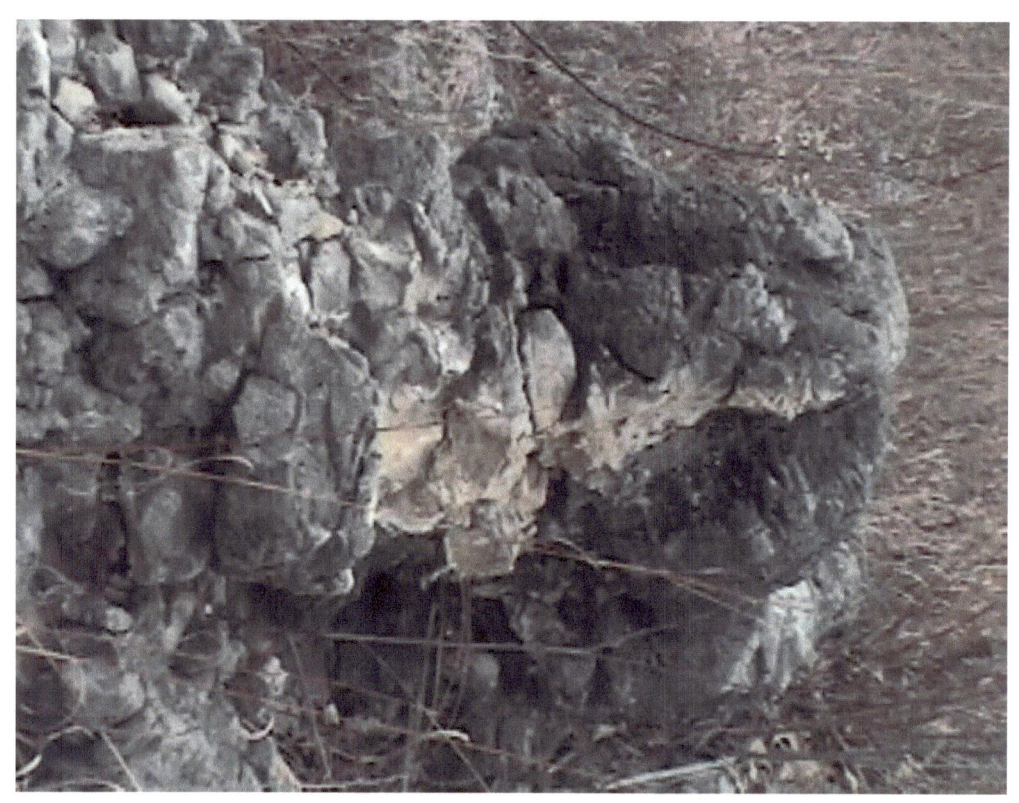

Rocky Foundation

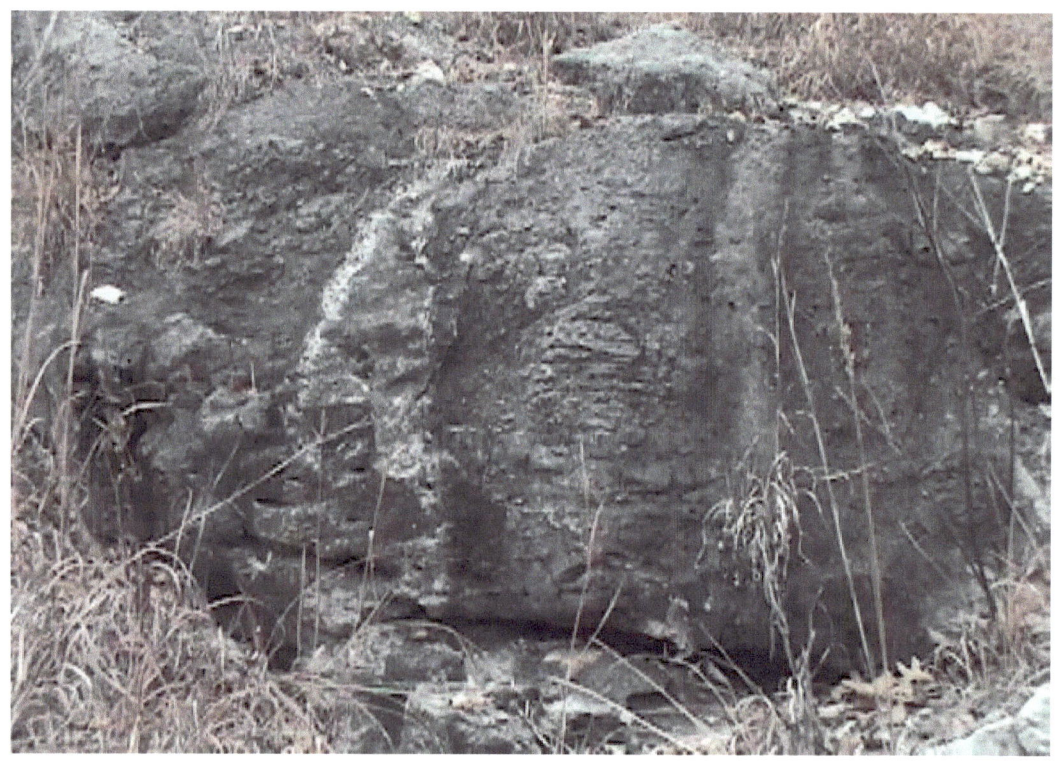

Solid

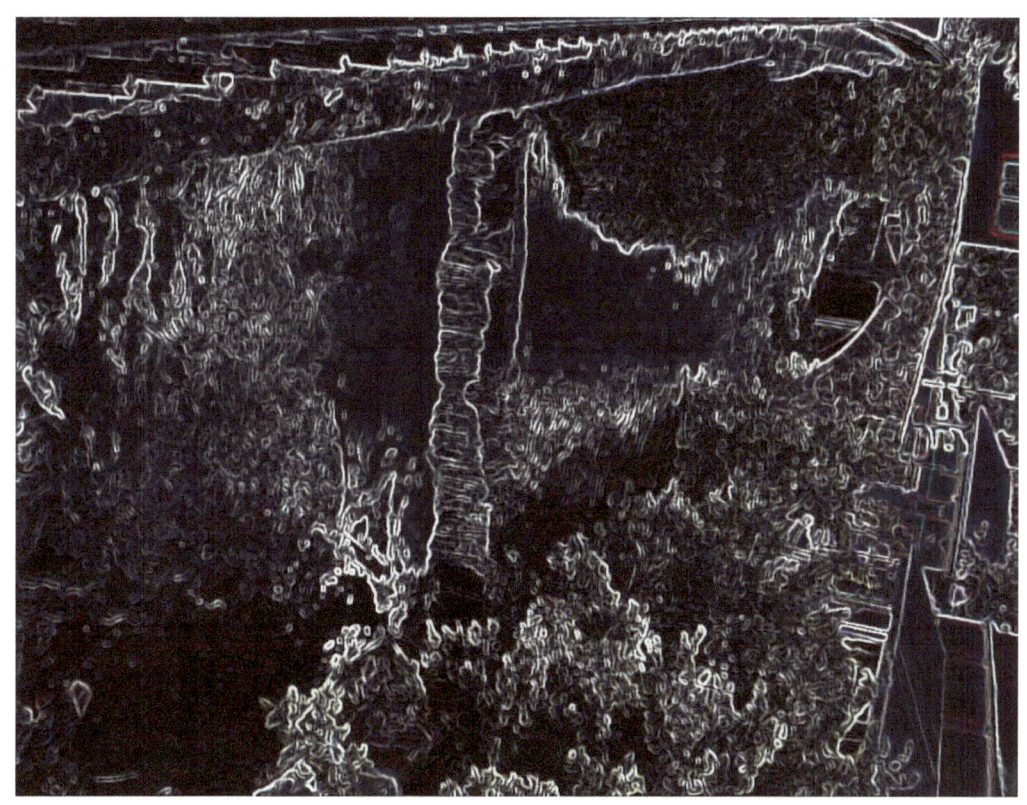

Tapping Lines of Movements

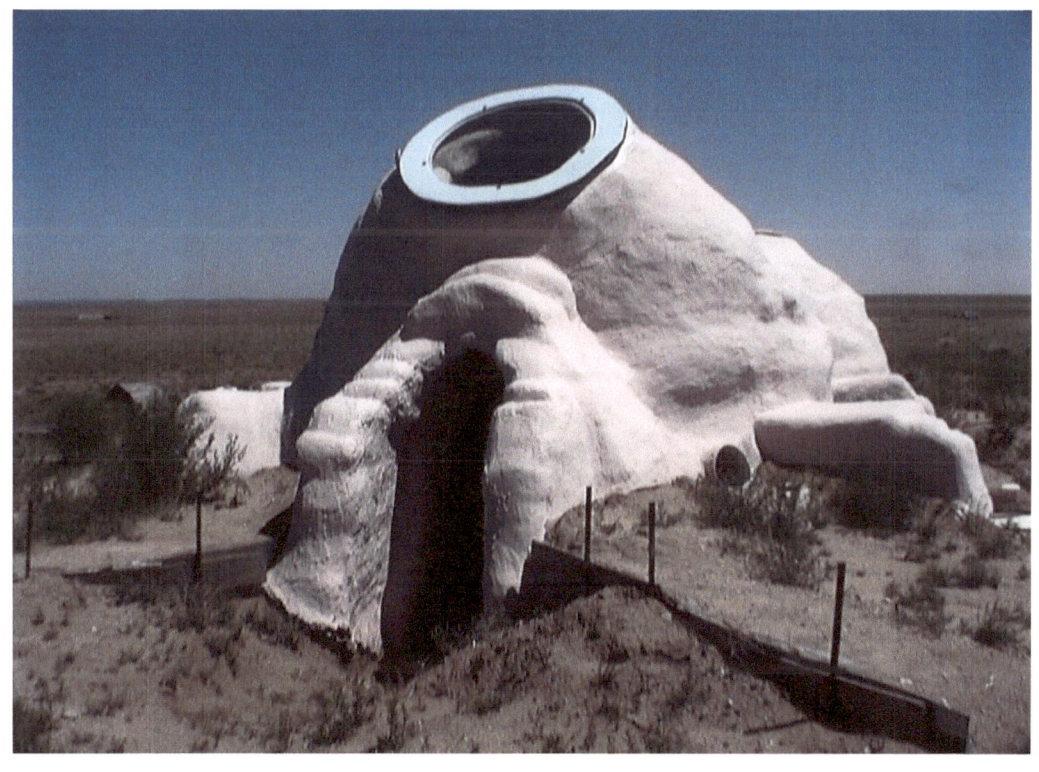

Final Destination of Home

www.ingramcontent.com/pod-product-compliance
Lightning Source LLC
Chambersburg PA
CBHW040057250526
45473CB00043B/1815